THE ROMANS

Anita Ganeri

STARGAZER BOOKS
Mankato, Minnesota

How to use this book

The key below shows the separate subject areas in this book. Included is information about language and literature, science and math, history, geography, and the Arts.

Introduction

The story of the Roman Empire begins with its growth from a group of tiny villages into one of the world's greatest empires, and ends with its collapse. At its height, the Empire controlled half of Europe, much of the Middle East, and parts of North Africa. This book provides the historical background to the Roman Empire and links it with information on various topics.

© Aladdin Books Ltd 2010

Created and produced by
Aladdin Books Ltd

First published in 2010
by Stargazer Books,
distributed by
Black Rabbit Books
P.O. Box 3263
Mankato, MN 56002

Printed in the United States

Design   Omnipress Ltd
Designer   Vivian Foster
Illustrators Sergio Momo,
              David Burroughs,
              David Russell

The author, Anita Ganeri, M.A., has written many books for children on history, natural history, and other topics.

The historical consultant, Dr. Anne Millard, has written many books for children on history and archaeology.

Library of Congress Cataloging-in-Publication Data

*Ganeri, Anita, 1961-
  The Romans / Anita Ganeri.
    p. cm. -- (All about ancient peoples)
Includes bibliographical references and index.
ISBN 978-1-59604-206-3 (alk. paper)
1. Rome--Civilization--Juvenile literature. I. Title.
DG77.G36 2009
937--dc22*

                    2008016508

Geography

The symbol of planet Earth shows where geographical facts and activities are included. These sections look at the extent of the Roman Empire at its height.

Language and literature

An open book is the sign for activities that involve language. These will explore how words are derived from the Latin language. Activities also include looking at some Roman myths and legends.

Science and math

The microscope symbol indicates science information or a science or math project. Topics covered include how the Romans developed a system of central heating.

History

The sign of the scroll and hourglass shows where historical information is given. These sections explore key figures and events in the history of Rome, and examine the impact of Roman culture on society today.

Social history

The symbol of a family shows where information about social history is given. These sections look into the everyday lives of the Romans. Topics include what the Romans wore and what they ate.

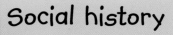

Arts, crafts, and music

This symbol showing a sheet of music and art tools signals arts, crafts, or musical activities. There are many fun ways of recreating Roman artefacts. Projects include making a theater mask and your own mosaic.

Contents

Kingdom to Republic

Rome began as a group of villages built on seven hills beside the Tiber River in Italy. At first, it was ruled by kings. In 509 BC, King Tarquin the Proud was driven out and Rome became a Republic. It was then governed by two consuls, elected each year by the Senate (see page 14). By 264 BC, Rome had overpowered its neighbors in Italy and begun its conquest abroad.

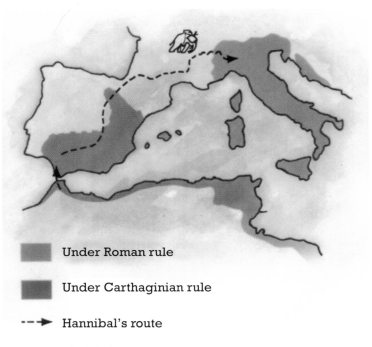

▨ Under Roman rule

▨ Under Carthaginian rule

--→ Hannibal's route

The Punic Wars

Between 264-146 BC, Rome waged war with Carthage, a powerful trading city in North Africa. In 218 BC, the Carthaginian general Hannibal led an army of 35,000 men and 37 elephants over the Alps into Italy. However, Carthage was eventually defeated in 146 BC.

Romulus and Remus

The traditional date for the founding of Rome is given as 753 BC. Legend says that the city was founded by a man called Romulus. He and his twin brother, Remus, had been brought up by a she-wolf. The brothers later quarreled, Remus was killed, and Romulus became the first king of Rome.

Civilizations

Greek civilization influenced many aspects of the developing Roman culture. Greek styles of art and architecture, such as those used in the Parthenon, below, were adapted by the Romans to suit their own purposes. The Romans greatly admired Greek methods of teaching and education. Slaves were often brought to Rome from Greece to work as teachers. As the Romans grew more powerful, they in turn began to influence other civilizations.

Julius Caesar was elected consul in 59 BC. In 49 BC, he defeated his rivals and seized power as a dictator. Caesar introduced social reform, but behaved too much like a king for many senators. On March 15, 44 BC, he was murdered. This resulted in Civil War, which led to the downfall of the Republic.

The Julian calendar

Julius Caesar introduced the Julian calendar in 46 BC. It is the basis of our modern calendar. Previously, the calendar had consisted of 355 days, divided into 12 months. To make the calendar more accurate, the Romans added 22 or 23 days every other year. This system was not always followed correctly. Caesar added 90 days to the year 46 BC to bring his new calendar into line. The Julian calendar was in common use until the 1500s, when the Gregorian calendar became more popular.

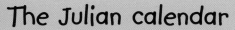

Civil wars

The success of the Roman expansion abroad caused many problems in Rome. During the wars with Carthage, local farmers had been recruited into the army, and their farms suffered from neglect or military destruction. When the wars ended, the farmers could not afford to repair the damage and were forced to give up their land to rich landowners. Many flocked to the cities, while leading citizens struggled for power. Civil wars erupted and the old Republic crumbled.

The Early Empire

In 27 BC, Julius Caesar's great-nephew, Octavian, emerged as the victor of the civil wars that had broken out after Caesar's death. Octavian restored peace and stability to Rome. Keen not to be seen as a king, he established himself as Rome's first emperor—a military title. He also took the title "Augustus," which means "revered" in Latin.

43 AD Conquest of southern Britain

60–61 AD Boudicca revolts against severity of Roman rule in Britain.

48 BC Caesar takes Gaul, which remains an important trading point throughout Empire.

After 30 BC, Greeks from Egypt settle in Nimes.

84 AD Northernmost advance

9 AD Three Roman legions suffer defeat at Teutoburger forest, in Germany.

101-106 AD Roman army under Trajan crosses the Danube River on a bridge of boats and conquers Dacia.

80 AD Colosseum opened by Titus.

64 AD Great fire of Rome

c.33 BC Tension between Mark Antony and Octavian leads to civil war.

Famous aqueduct built at Segovia. It stretches nearly half a mile (over 800 m.)

53–117 AD Trajan born in Spain.

Pompey destroys pirates in the Mediterranean Sea. Murdered in 48 BC.

79 AD Vesuvius erupts, totally destroying Pompeii.

31 BC Sea battle at Actium; Octavian beats Antony and Cleopatra.

New city of Leptis Magna developed under Augustus.

Wild animals shipped to Rome for public games.

Expeditions undertaken to explore the Sahara.

BC to AD

Yearly dates today are based on the birth of Christ. The years before his birth (BC means Before Christ) are counted backward. For example, Caesar was murdered in 44 BC and Augustus became emperor 17 years later, in 27 BC. The years after the birth of Christ are counted forward. AD stands for *anno Domini* (in the year of our Lord). Augustus died in 14 AD. How many years did he rule? *(Note: 1 AD follows directly after 1 BC.)*

Importance of the countryside

Although the Roman Empire was famous for its magnificent cities, much of its wealth came from the countryside. Most people lived off the land, and farming was one of the Empire's most important industries. Among the crops grown were grapes for making wine, and olives which were used for olive oil, as well as eating. As the Empire expanded, farming became more efficient and productive.

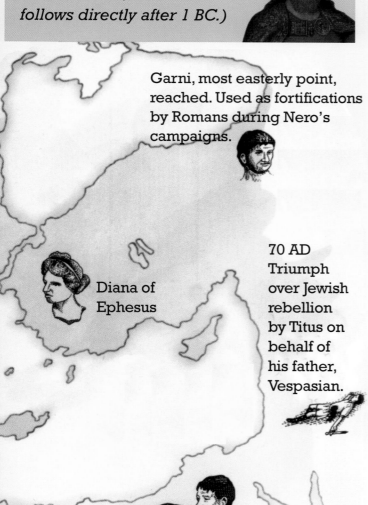

Garni, most easterly point, reached. Used as fortifications by Romans during Nero's campaigns.

Diana of Ephesus

70 AD Triumph over Jewish rebellion by Titus on behalf of his father, Vespasian.

30 BC Antony and his lover, the Egyptian Queen Cleopatra, commit suicide. Octavian becomes sole ruler of the Roman world.

The first emperors

Augustus ruled from 27 BC until 14 AD.

He was succeeded by his stepson, Tiberius, who ruled until 37 AD. Gaius (also known as Caligula) was the next emperor. Caligula's extravagant lifestyle and his cruelty

Augustus

made him very unpopular. He was murdered in 41 AD.

Claudius

Tiberius's nephew, Claudius, ruled from 41-54 AD. Nero came next, but he killed himself in 68 AD. The rule was then passed to Vespasian, the founder of the Flavian dynasty, in 69 AD.

Nero

Vespasian

He was followed by Titus (79-81 AD), Domitian (81-96 AD), and Nerva (96-98 AD). Trajan ruled from 91-117 AD, followed by Hadrian (117-138 AD).

Trajan

The Roman Army

The rapid expansion and incredible success of the Roman Empire was largely due to the Roman army. It was first formed to defend the city of Rome, but it went on to conquer a vast empire. The early Roman army was made up of volunteers, but General Marius reorganized it into a well trained and better equipped force.

Tribune

Legatus

Emperor

A legionary's uniform

Over a woolen tunic, a legionary wore a breast-plate made of metal strips, scales, or rings. He also had a helmet of leather or metal. During cold weather he was given a thick, hooded cloak, called a *Birrus britannicus*. A foot soldier was armed with a short sword, two metal-tipped javelins, and a rectangular shield of wood and leather. On the march, a legionary had to carry all his heavy equipment on his back.

Copy of shield

Emperor   Legatus   Tribune   Centurion   Signifer   Legionary   Auxiliary

Left: The order of ranks in the Roman army

A Roman legion

A Roman legion was divided up into separate units. Ten sections of eight men made up a century. Six centuries made a cohort (480 men), and there were ten cohorts in a legion. There were also about 120 cavalrymen attached to each legion. Each legion had as its standard an eagle, the symbol of the Roman Empire.

Cohorts

Cavalry

Signifer

Aquifer

Auxiliary cavalry

Fighting talk

Many of the words that we use today come from Latin.

A *corduroy* consisted of logs laid side by side to form the foundations of a rampart. The pattern of lines of corduroy cloth resembles the logs.

A *praefectus* was a high official in Rome. Today, the word prefect means someone with authority.

Gladius is the Latin word for sword. From it come the words gladiator and gladioli.

Ballista is the Latin word for catapult. Today, the word ballistics is used in connection with weapons.

Tortoise technique

The Romans devised many new military techniques. The "tortoise" formation involved soldiers holding their shields above their heads as protection against arrows, stones, and other missiles hurled by the enemy. The raised shields resembled the pattern on a tortoise's shell and offered a similar protection, hence its name. The Romans also used assault towers and battering rams as a way of storming enemy territory.

9

Roman Society

Roman society was highly organized. People were divided into citizens and slaves. Citizens themselves were divided into different ranks, and had special rights and duties that were denied to noncitizens. By 212 AD all free members of the Empire were allowed to become Roman citizens, but slaves could not.

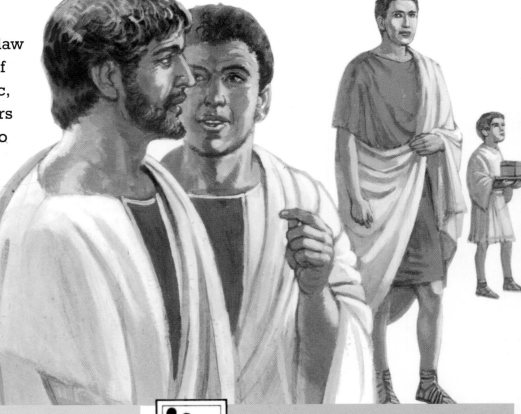

The Senate was the main law and policy making body of Rome. During the Republic, the senators were members of aristocratic families. Two consuls were elected to head the Senate. Poorer citizens eventually won the right to stand for high office.

The toga was a sign of Roman citizenship. Senators wore togas with a purple stripe.

Portraiture

Roman portraits were usually carved from marble. They were meant to be an accurate representation of the subject, whether with beautiful, unattractive, or unusual features.

The family

The family was ruled by a *paterfamilias* (father), who had complete authority over his wife, children, and slaves. When he died, each of his sons became head of a new family that was related to the old one by name. This chain of families was known as a clan.

Spartacus and his slaves

Slaves had no rights or status. They were owned by Roman citizens, or by the state. Many were treated cruelly by their masters, and there were several rebellions by discontented slaves. The most famous one was led by Spartacus. He formed an army of slaves in 73 BC, which had over 90,000 members. Spartacus's army achieved many victories until it was defeated by the Roman army in 71 BC.

There were three classes of Roman citizen. **Patricians** were the wealthiest and most aristocratic. **Equites** were rich business people. Ordinary citizens were called **plebeians** or "commoners."

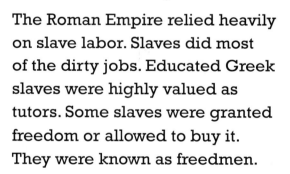

The Roman Empire relied heavily on slave labor. Slaves did most of the dirty jobs. Educated Greek slaves were highly valued as tutors. Some slaves were granted freedom or allowed to buy it. They were known as freedmen.

The business classes

The period of early Empire was one of great prosperity, in which trade flourished. A powerful middle class of businessmen, traders, and bankers emerged, called equites. They were responsible for the wealth of goods that flooded into the Empire (see map). Luxury goods, such as spices, Indian cotton, and precious stones traveled to Rome by ship, and silks from China came along the Silk Road. Egyptian wheat arrived in huge galleys.

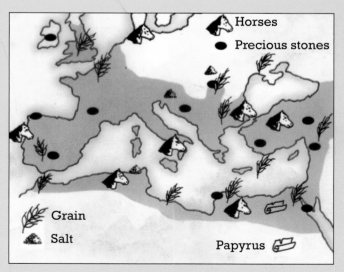

Horses
Precious stones
Grain
Salt
Papyrus

The Pax Romana

Emperor Trajan ruled from 98 to 117 AD. During his reign the Empire reached its greatest size with the conquest of large areas of land in the east. His successor, Hadrian, concentrated on improving the way the Empire was run. This was the time of the Pax Romana (Roman Peace).

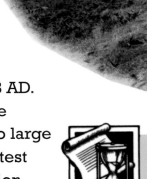

Hadrian ruled Rome from 117 to 138 AD. He spent much of his time touring the Empire and decided it had grown too large to defend. He gave up some of the latest conquests, reformed the administration, and strengthened the army.

Coinage

The first Roman coin was used in about 280 BC. Coins were originally minted to pay soldiers' wages and make the collection of taxes easier. Gradually, they began to be used all over the Empire and replaced the bartering system in which people traded with goods, not money. Under Augustus, all coins were given a fixed value. The coin shown here was minted during the reign of Hadrian.

Roman numerals

Roman numerals are written from left to right and added together to give a number. Thus, 2,650 is written MMDCL— MM (2,000), DC (500 + 100 = 600), L (50).

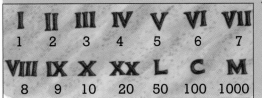

I	II	III	IV	V	VI	VII
1	2	3	4	5	6	7

VIII	IX	X	XX	L	C	M
8	9	10	20	50	100	1000

Write out some other numerals.

Fortified walls were built at Hadrian's command in Germany, Numidia in Africa, and in Britain. The one shown below is in Britain and is known as Hadrian's Wall. It is the best preserved of all the walls.

The map (inset) shows the Empire at its greatest extent. Roman provinces are marked in brown.

Making mosaics

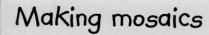

Mosaics were made from tiny pieces of colored stone or tile, and used to decorate walls, floors, and pavements. They showed scenes from mythology or daily life, or abstract patterns. You can make a mosaic like the one below using paper or modeling clay. On a large piece of paper, sketch the design you want to use. Cut out the different colors you need and glue them onto the design, working on one area at a time. Use tiny triangles and squares to give the effect of curved lines.

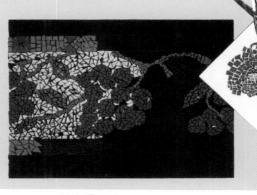

Medicine

The Romans gained much of their medical knowledge from the Greeks, and in particular from the Greek doctor, Hippocrates. Roman medicine was a mixture of science and religion. Plants were used in medicines, and operations were performed without anesthetic. Ancient iron and bronze medical instruments (pictured) have been found. People also believed in the healing powers of the gods.

Central heating

The hypocaust system was a form of underfloor central heating which was invented in the first century AD. Buildings were specially built with spaces between their inner and outer walls, and beneath the floors. A fire was lit and the heat was allowed to flow into the cavities. The hypocaust was used mainly to heat the bathhouses (see page 17).

Fire   Wall cavity   Floor

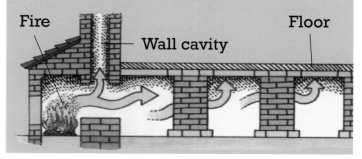

Under Roman Rule

During the Republic, the Senate was the main law body in Rome. In 450 BC, however, the plebeians rebelled against the senators who held power. They demanded that the laws of Rome should be written down, so that new laws could not be invented and used against them. This body of law was called the Twelve Tables. During the Roman Empire, the Emperor was the supreme ruler.

The Justinian Code

The Twelve Tables listed laws governing ownership of property, family matters, types of punishment, and so on. They were constantly being added to. In 528 AD, Emperor Justinian set about putting the huge mass of Roman law into order and his work became known as the Justinian Code.

Trials

As today, Roman criminals were tried by a jury. In serious cases, the jury consisted of up to 75 citizens, and a lawyer was appointed to represent the accused person. Trials were held in huge government buildings, called basilicas. It was permissible to torture slaves to make them give evidence.

Legacy of Roman government

Many modern governments are based on the Roman model. The United States adopted many Roman ideas in their creation of the Constitution. Words such as *republic, senate,* and *capitol* are all taken directly from Rome.

Abraham Lincoln (right) was the U.S. President from 1861-1865.

Elect a government

You can hold your own elections at school for some of the positions of Roman government. Two *consuls* must be appointed to control the Senate and command the armies. Four *aediles* are needed to look after streets, markets, and public buildings, and to organize public games. There are also 20 financial administrators, called *quaestores*, and eight *praetores*, or senior judges. Finally, two *censores* were elected every five years to oversee any changes in the membership of the Senate.

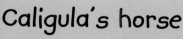

Caligula's horse

Caligula ruled Rome from 37-41 AD. After a few months as Emperor, he suffered from an illness that affected his mind. He claimed to be a god, and made his horse a senator!

Building Feats

The Romans were superb engineers and architects and many of their buildings survive today. They include bridges and aqueducts, public baths and, of course, roads. By 200 AD, the Roman army had built an amazing 52,800 miles (85,000 km) of roads. The first main road, the Via Appia, was built in 312 BC, and stretched from Rome to Capua. The Romans also built sewers and central heating systems, and invented the first type of concrete. It was made from volcanic rocks and rubble.

A classical style

Roman architecture was heavily influenced by the Greeks. The Romans excelled at building on a grand scale. They used columns, arches, vaults, and domes to create an impression of physical perfection and splendor.

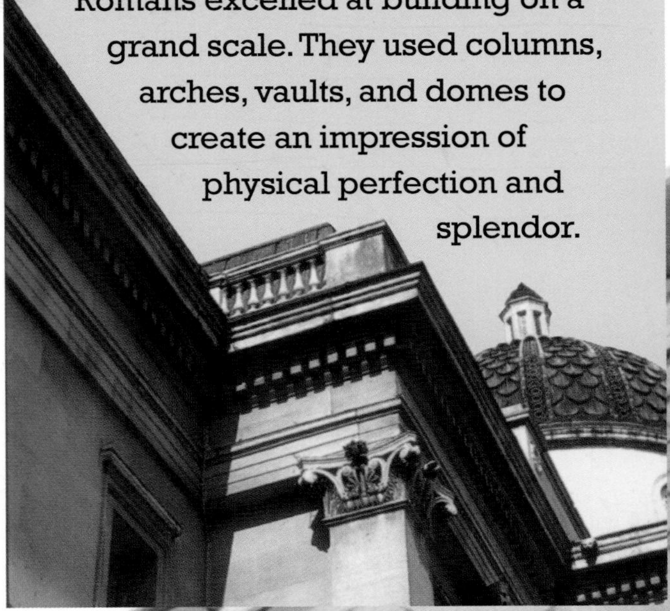

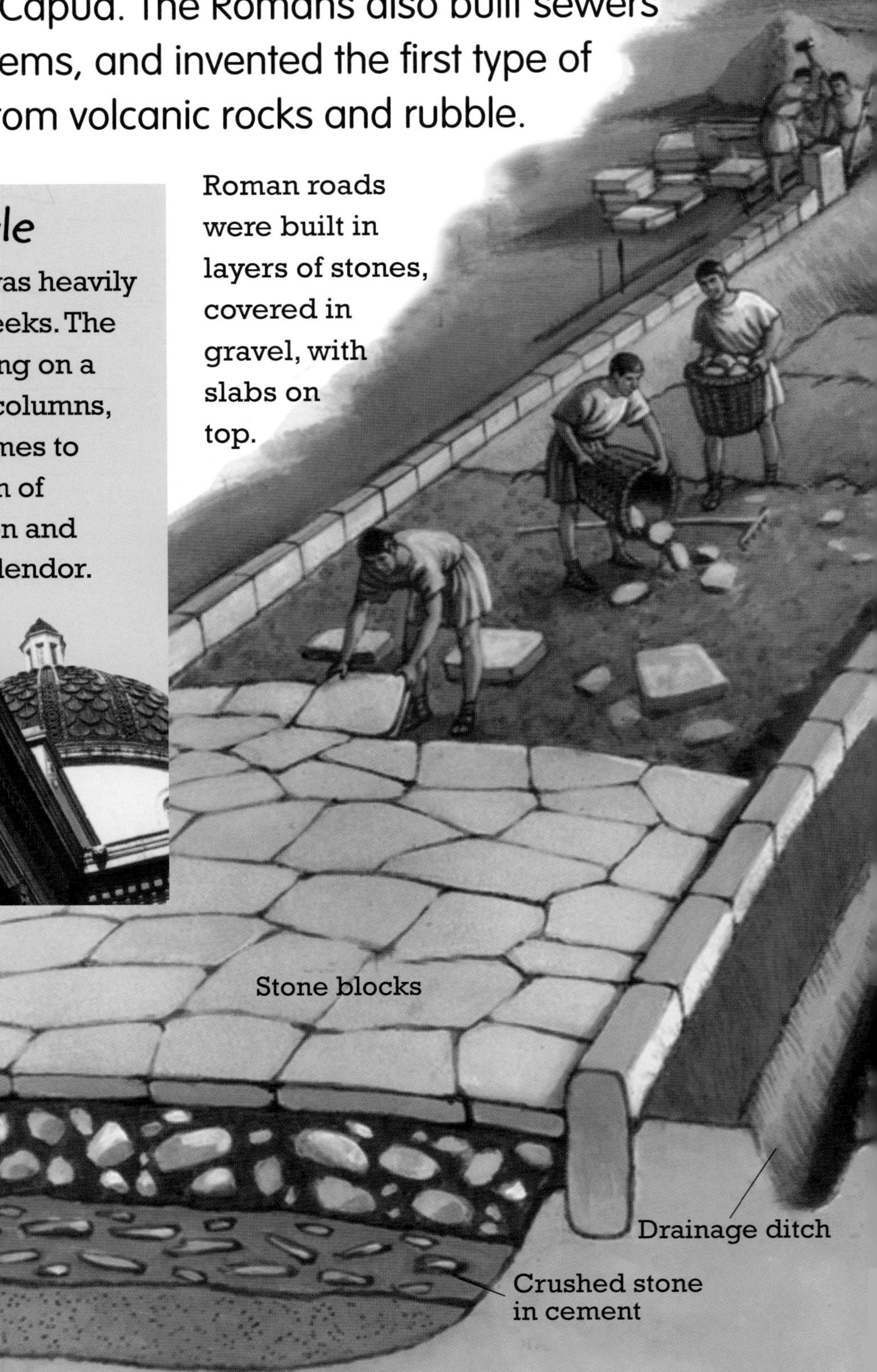

Roman roads were built in layers of stones, covered in gravel, with slabs on top.

Stone blocks

Stone slabs in cement

Drainage ditch

Sand

Crushed stone in cement

16

The word mile comes from *mille*, the Latin word for thousand. A Roman mile was 1,000 paces (1,600 yards/1,500 m).

Hot air

Roman baths in Bath, England

Few Roman houses had bathrooms, so people went to the public baths. Here they could bathe, have a massage, and chat to their friends. The baths were heated from underground. Slaves stoked large fires which sent hot air under the raised floors.

Building innovations

The development of the arch enabled the Romans to build many of their famous bridges and aqueducts. Arches were extremely heavy and had to be supported by pillars and buttresses. This helped to distribute their weight, and made the arches incredibly strong. They were built from whatever stone was available. For important buildings, marble was used. The development of concrete made from sand, stone, and water meant that huge, multistoried buildings such as the Colosseum could be built.

Wooden frame

A cutaway of the Colosseum

Town planning

Roman towns were built on a grid pattern. At the center of each town was a forum (marketplace), a basilica (town hall), and several temples. Around the town a holy boundary was marked by massive walls. Outside the city, the roads were lined with gravestones, as burials were forbidden within the holy boundary.

Rich and Poor

Family life was very important to the Romans. The father was head of the household and was called *paterfamilias*. The daily running of the house was left to the women. They were not encouraged to go out to work, but instead were expected to raise the children and attend to the domestic duties. There were huge differences between the daily lives of rich and poor in the Roman Empire (see below).

Wealthy housing

Most rich Romans had both a city home, called a *domus*, and a country house. The walls and floors of a *domus* were often decorated with beautiful mosaics and frescoes, although there was little furniture. Lamps burning olive oil provided light.

Cooking on a makeshift stove

Waste thrown into street

Atrium

Impluvium

Store

Public lavatories

Fire company

Poor housing

Poor city people lived in crowded blocks of apartments, called *insulae*. The *insulae* were badly built fire hazards. The ground floor was usually occupied by a row of stores. The upper floors usually had no heating, sewers, or running water. People had to fetch water from fountains in the street. Most had no kitchen. People bought hot food from stores. Any attempt at cooking increased the threat of fire. Augustus established a fire service in Rome, with seven companies, valled *vigiles*, with 1,000 men in each.

After lunch

Everyone, whether rich or poor, stopped for lunch at noon. Lunch was followed by a short rest, called a siesta, which is still taken in many Mediterranean countries. The wealthy did not work after lunch. Their afternoons were spent relaxing at the baths and meeting friends. They often invited people home for a long, leisurely meal in the evening. The poor people worked until dusk, then ate dinner and went to bed when it got dark. Wealthy women often spent their days reading (right).

Strigils were used for scraping oil and dirt off the skin before bathing.

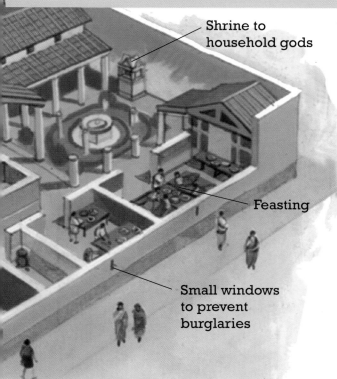

Shrine to household gods

Feasting

Small windows to prevent burglaries

Crime and punishment

Assassinations, pickpocketing, and burglaries were common during the Empire. The streets of Rome were policed by groups of men under the control of the City Prefect. Criminals were divided into two categories: *honestiores* and *humiliores*. Humiliores were usually poorer and given the worst punishments. Offenders could be exiled or forced to work under harsh conditions.

The message on this mosaic reads: "Beware of the dog!"

Food and feasting

Wealthy Romans sometimes held lavish feasts for their guests. On the menu there were numerous dishes, such as eggs, lettuce, snails, or oysters. There may also have been delicacies like lark or dormouse, with plenty of olives, wine, and figs. The Romans did not use forks or knives. Guests ate with their hands, which were wiped by slaves. Wine was mixed with water and drunk out of glass or silver goblets. Honey was added to the food and wine to sweeten it. People reclined on three couches arranged around a table in the *triclinium* (dining room).

Entertainment

Public games, paid for by the Emperor, were an important part of Roman life. There were three types of "games" or *ludi*—gladiator fights and wild beast shows, chariot races, and theater plays. In Rome, gladiator fights were held in the Colosseum. They were hugely popular. People flocked to watch men fight to the death. Gladiators were usually slaves or criminals. Some female slaves were even trained as gladiators.

A deadly sport

Gladiator fights were spectacular and usually held in the afternoon. Fights were held between different types of gladiator—a *retiarius*, armed with only a trident and a net, might fight a Samnite with a shield and sword, or a spear. Gladiators also fought wild animals. The gladiator's fate was decided by the Emperor himself.

Fun and games

The games played by Roman children were similar to those played today. A game like marbles was played with walnuts. *Tali* (knucklebones) was played with pieces of pottery and was similar to dice. Board games were also popular. Make a Roman version of the board game Parcheesi based on a chariot race. Use different colored counters for the team.

Marbles

Walnut

Whip top

Knucklebones (*tali*)

Minera

One of the highlights of the Games was the beast show (*minera*). At great expense antelopes, elephants, Indian tigers, and rhinos were shipped back to Rome to fight in the arena. Thousands of animals and humans died in these violent contests.

A trip to the Circus

In Rome, chariot races were held in the huge Circus Maximus. There were four teams—Reds, Greens, Blues, and Whites. A race consisted of as many as 12 chariots, running seven laps of the track (a distance of about five miles/eight km). The drivers needed extreme skill to keep their horses under control.

Sometimes naval battles were held in the Circus Maximus, and the arena would be specially flooded for this purpose.

Making music

Music and dancing were an important part of Roman culture. They took place at the theater, at public games, and at some religious festivals. Competitions were held to see who could blow the longest note! Many Roman instruments were of Greek origin. Lyres, *below*, were very popular and often associated with the gods.

Theater masks

All the parts in a Roman play were played by male actors, even the female ones! To help the audience distinguish between the different characters, the actors wore masks on stage. Try making a Roman mask from papier-mâché. Decorate your mask according to the type of character you are playing, with a smiling face for comedy and a sad face for tragedy.

21

Gods and Religion

The Romans worshipped a great many gods and spirits—about 30,000 in all. These included the major gods and goddesses, such as Jupiter, the chief god, Neptune, god of the sea, Venus, goddess of love, and Minerva, goddess of wisdom and war. Each household also worshipped its own protective spirits—the Lares, Penates, and Manes. After Augustus's death, the Emperors were also considered as gods. People all over the Empire were allowed to worship their own local gods, as long as they paid homage to the Roman gods.

One of the household Lares, the guardian of houses

Household gods
Every Roman house had its own shrine to the household gods (Lares), called a *Lararium*, where worship took place daily. The family offered gifts such as wine, bread, and fruit. Outside the home, people worshipped the Roman gods in shrines and temples (right).

Festivals

Roman festivals were regarded as holy days (holidays), during which people did not have to work. Under Augustus, there were at least 115 public holidays. These festivals were usually celebrated with games and races.

The rites of Bona Dea was held in early December and it was only for women.

Compitalia was in early January. *Parilia* was in April, when people danced around bonfires.

Religious persecution

During the Empire, many Romans felt the empty rituals of the state religion could no longer meet their spiritual needs. Foreign cults such as those of Mithras, Isis, and Cybele encouraged their followers to take part in ceremonies. Christianity was not tolerated by the Romans. Its followers refused to worship the state gods and were often cruelly persecuted.

Vestal virgins

Vesta was the Goddess of the Hearth. The six Vestal Virgins had to perform symbolic household duties for the state. This included tending the fire dedicated to Vesta which burned in her temple in the forum. The Virgins had to remain unmarried for 30 years. Those who did not were buried alive.

Offerings and sacrifices

People tried to discover the will of the gods with sacrifices. Sheep, chickens, bulls, and pigs were the main sacrificial animals. The priests removed their innards and read them to discover the gods' intentions.

Looking heavenward

The positions of the stars and the planets at the time of a person's birth were considered very significant by the Romans.

Mercury

Many of the stars and planets were named after Roman and Greek gods and goddesses. Mercury was named after the messenger of the gods, who was also the god of trade and thieves. Venus was the goddess of love and beauty. Mars was the god of war. Jupiter was the king of the gods. Can you find out who the other planets were named after?

Jupiter

Venus

Ceremonies

Special ceremonies marked important events in the lives of all Romans. A newborn baby was placed at its father's feet. The father raised the child in his arms as a sign of acceptance into the family. Funerals were very grand affairs, with professional mourners hired to wail over the body. In Republican times, death masks and mourning robes were worn. This practice was stopped during the Empire. Roman marriages were usually arranged.

The Roman Language

The Romans spoke a language called Latin. It provided a common language across the Empire, and enabled people from far and wide to communicate with each other. Greek was also widely spoken in the east. Many of our everyday words have Latin origins, and the modern alphabets used in western Europe are based on the Latin alphabet below. During the Middle Ages, Latin was the main language of the Church and scholarship. It remained the official language of the Roman Catholic Church well into the 20th century.

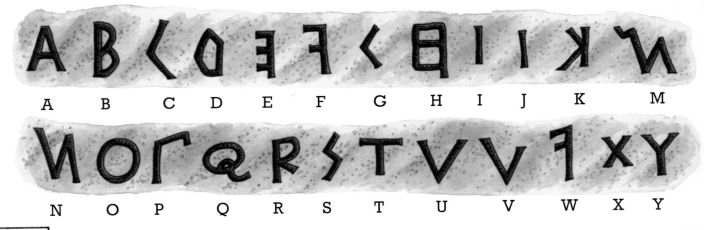

A B C D E F G H I J K M

N O P Q R S T U V W X Y

Schooling

Only children whose parents could afford it received an education. From the age of six, Roman boys attended a kind of elementary school called a *ludus*. Rich children were accompanied by a slave called a *pedagogue*, who supervised the child throughout the school day. Although most children left school at 11, the wealthy ones went on to attend a higher school, or *grammaticus*.

Here, one of the main aims was to prepare teenage boys for a life in politics, the law, or public speaking. Girls received only a very basic education, after which they learned how to be wives and mothers.

Young boys stayed with their mothers until they were old enough to go to school. Girls stayed at home, where they were taught skills such as weaving and spinning by their mothers.

Writers and poets

There were many famous Roman writers and poets, such as Virgil, Livy, Cicero, Catullus, and Pliny. One of the most famous Roman works is Virgil's epic poem, the *Aeneid* (illustrated right). It is the story of Aeneas, a legendary Trojan prince. When Troy was destroyed by the Greeks, Aeneas escaped to Italy, where his descendants founded Rome.

Writing

Writing at school was done on a piece of wood which was covered with wax. A pointed metal pen, called a stylus, was used to scratch letters and figures onto the wax. To make a writing tablet, chop up several candles into a bowl. Melt the wax over a pan of boiling water (get an adult to help you with this bit), and pour it into a shallow tray. Let it cool. Use a knitting needle point or blunt pencil to write on your tablet.

Maturus and Grippus

The lives of wealthy and poor children were very different. Maturus is poor and Grippus is rich. In diary form, describe what a day in the life of each boy would be like. For example, if Maturus is poor, he will not be able to read and write. Describe a visit to the store, where Maturus has to buy his dinner. What is home like? Grippus, on the other hand, is educated. Who takes him to school each day? What kinds of things does he learn? What games does he play?

Genus

Latin names are used for scientific classifications. Below are some Latin names used in natural history.

The genus (group) *equus* consists of horses, asses, and zebra.

Felix is the Latin name for the cat family. From it comes the word feline, which means catlike.

Bovis is the Latin term for cattle. Today, the word bovine means resembling oxen or cows.

The End of the Empire

Toward the end of the 2nd century AD, the Roman Empire began to face problems. Barbarian tribes started invading Roman territory. The army grew weaker and were unable to control the situation. At home, rival emperors squabbled over power. In 285 AD, Emperor Diocletian divided the Empire into two parts—east and west, each with its own emperor. But rising prices and taxes and even more invasions led to the collapse in the west. In 476 AD, the last western emperor, Romulus Augustus, was deposed.

The Angles, Jutes, and Saxons moved in and took over the Roman Provinces in Britain.

The Franks invaded Gaul, giving their name to modern-day France.

The Huns came from eastern Asia. They invaded the lands of the Vandals, Ostrogoths, and Visigoths.

ROMAN EMPIRE

The Burgundians were from Northern Europe. In 406 AD, they set up their own kingdom in Germania.

The Ostrogoths In the 370s AD, the Ostrogoths moved westward to escape the Huns. They overran Italy in 489 AD.

The Vandals were of Scandinavian descent. In 409 AD, they took control of Roman provinces in North Africa and Spain.

The Visigoths settled in Dacia in the 200s AD. In 410 AD, led by the Goth chief, Alaric, they sacked the city of Rome.

The Lombards In 568 AD, the Lombards conquered Northern Italy and set up the kingdom of Lombardy.

Overspending

Toward the end of the Empire, vast sums of money were spent on lavish projects and games, which led to massive inflation. The currency collapsed, prices rose, and taxation was heavy.

The coming of Christianity

In the fourth century AD, the Christian Church became more powerful and began to influence the way in which the Empire was run. When the barbarians started invading, it was Christian bishops, not army generals, who organized the defense against them.

This mosaic is in the Santa Sophia church, Istanbul.

Civil wars

During the 3rd century AD, it became clear that the Empire could no longer be effectively controlled from a central authority in Rome. A series of civil wars erupted between 235 and 284 AD, which drastically weakened the army's power. Struggles among army generals for control of the Empire further weakened the Empire's defenses. When Rome was attacked from the East by the newly-formed and powerful Persian Empire and from the North by the Germans, the collapse of the Roman Empire seemed inevitable.

Coins minted at this time lost their value so quickly that new ones of higher values had to be minted.

The remains of the Empire

The Emperor Constantine began reuniting the Empire after its split into east and west by Diocletian. In 330 AD, Constantine moved his court from Rome to Byzantium. There, he founded a new capital city to rival the former power and splendor of Rome. It was called Constantinople (modern-day Istanbul). The Byzantine Empire survived until 1453 AD, when Constantinople was finally captured by the Turks.

The Legacy of Rome

Even today, over 1,500 years after the decline of the Byzantine Empire, Rome still has an enormous influence over our lives. Many of our buildings were copied from the Roman style of architecture. Our legal and political systems can be traced back to Roman times. There is also a huge quantity of historical evidence, from literature and coins to surviving roads and aqueducts, to keep the memory of Rome well and truly alive.

The Radcliffe Camera is a library in Oxford, England. Its architect, James Gibbs (1683–1754), modeled it on a Roman basilica. The dome, the pillars, and the ornate, classical style are reminiscent of many of the magnificent buildings of the Roman Empire. Several major cities have been built on sites chosen by the Romans. For example, Londinium (modern-day London in England) was founded by the Romans in 43 AD as a seaport. Can you find any other examples of towns or cities that were built by the Romans, and that remain today?

The Roman revival, or Renaissance

In the early 15th century, writers, artists, sculptors, and architects began to draw inspiration from ancient Greece and Rome. Ruins were studied and statues were dug up. Ancient myths and legends inspired paintings such as the French artist Claude's depiction of Aeneas at Delos (right). Latin literature also influenced Renaissance writers.

The European Union flag

The period of the Roman Empire demonstrated the possibility of one government controlling large areas. Roman citizenship gave people a sense of identity. Today, the European Union can be seen to reflect ideals of unity, albeit with modern goals of a single monetary and taxation system and a central government.

Herbal medicine

For centuries, the healing properties of plants and herbs have been used by different cultures, including the Romans. Try growing your own herbs from seed in a garden path or in a small pot. Place them in a sunny, sheltered spot and remember to water them well. Some of the medicinal properties of herbs are listed below.

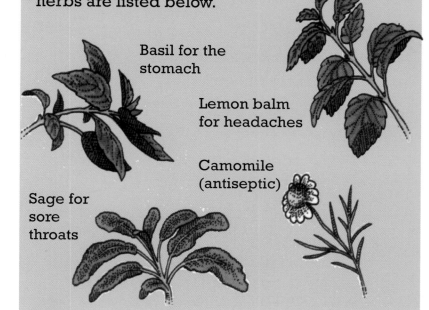

Basil for the stomach

Lemon balm for headaches

Camomile (antiseptic)

Sage for sore throats

Pompeii

Much of the evidence that we have today about ancient Rome comes from archaeological excavations in places such as Pompeii (below). The town has been well preserved under the volcanic ash that engulfed it in 79 AD. Its forum, basilica, theaters, temples, lavish villas, and tiny sleeping quarters offer a complete picture of Roman life.

The French Empire

The Imperial system used by the Romans was later copied by rulers of other European countries. The Frankish king, Charlemagne, revived the idea of the Roman Empire in the West. Called the Holy Roman Empire, it was destroyed by Napoleon Bonaparte. He modeled his own Empire on that of Rome and even called himself Emperor.

753 BC Traditional date for the founding of Rome.

520 Last king expelled from Rome; Republic formed.

49 Caesar returns to Rome and seizes power; civil war breaks out.

31 Victory for Octavian at the Battle of Actium.

27 Octavian becomes first Emperor and the Roman Empire begins.

c.5 Actual birth of Christ.

14 AD Augustus dies.

43 Roman conquest of southern Britain.

117 Death of Trajan; accession of Hadrian. Roman Empire at its greatest extent.

212 Roman citizenship granted to all free members of the Empire.

230s onward Wars with Persia. Barbarians begin invasions across Rhine and Danube.

253–268 Germanic barbarians invade the Empire.

284 Accession of Diocletian, who splits Empire into East and West.

312 Constantine becomes Emperor; reunites Empire from 324 onward.

313 Edict of Milan. Christianity tolerated within Empire.

410 Rome captured by Alaric the Goth; around this time, Roman rule ends in Britain.

476 Romulus Augustulus, last western Roman Emperor, deposed by Odovacar, a barbarian leader.

8000 BC

First hieroglyphs (picture writing) in Egypt c.3500 BC

Old Kingdom in Egypt 2686–2150 BC

Pyramids built in Egypt during Old Kingdom

Egyptian Middle Kingdom 2040–1640 BC

2000 BC

Reign of Tutankhamun—the boy pharoah c.1347–1339 BC

New Kingdom in Egypt 1552–1085 BC

Romulus and Remus found the city of Rome 753 BC

500 BC Roman Empire c.27 BC

Julius Caesar murdered 44 BC

Fall of the Roman Empire AD 476

Viking raids across western Europe AD 700s-1000s

AD 1000 First Crusade to recapture Holy Land from Muslims AD 1096

First mechanical clock AD 1386

The Aztec Empire in Central America AD 1300s-1521

AD c.1200-1532 The Inca Empire in South America

First cities—Jericho and Catal Hüyük 8000-5650 BC

Wheel invented by the Sumerians 3500-3000 BC

Rise of the Indus Valley civilization 2500-1700 BC

Early Minoan period in Crete begins c.2500 BC

Stonehenge in England built in phases c.3000-1500 BC

Shang Dynasty in China c.1766-1122 BC

Destruction of Knossos in Crete. End of the Minoan period c.1400 BC

Birth of Confucius 551 BC

Siddhartha Gautama, the Buddha c.500 BC

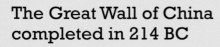

The Golden Age of Greece 479–431 BC

Alexander the Great conquers Persia, Syria, and Egypt c.333-330 BC

The Qin Dynasty in China 221-206 BC

The Great Wall of China completed in 214 BC

Samurai warriors of Japan AD 1100s-1850

The Plague, or Black Death, spreads in Europe AD 1300s

First mechanical printing press developed by Gutenberg in Germany in AD c.1450

Christopher Columbus lands in the Americas AD 1492.

Glossary

Aediles Roman government officials who looked after the streets, markets, and public buildings.

Augustus Honorary title given to the Emperor.

Basilica Large public building.

Censores Government officials.

Centurion Officer in charge of an army unit.

Consul The most senior official in the government.

Equites Rich business people.

Forum Large open space in the center of a Roman town.

Insulae Apartment blocks.

Legion An army unit.

Mosaic Pattern made of tiny pieces of glass or tile.

Paterfamilias Head of a Roman family—the father.

Patricians Richest Romans.

Pax Romana The "Roman Peace."

Plebeians Ordinary Romans.

Praetores Government officials who acted as senior judges.

Quaestores Government officials in charge of finance.

Senate Council of citizens that ruled Rome.

Index